# FROM ME TO YOU

## YDRATE **NELSON**

www.YdrateNelson.com

FROM ME TO YOU Volume 1

simplebooklet.com/frommetoyouvolume1

Scan QR Code and receive your **Digital Copy** of FROM ME TO YOU.

Scan QR Code and **Download Soundtrack** for FROM ME TO YOU.

F.R.O.M. M.E. T.O. Y.O.U. Volume 1

# The Poetic Express

Inspired by L.I.F.E.

Personal Stories, Essays, Poems,

& Creative Thoughts

Ydrate "The Motivator" Nelson, M. Ed

# The Poetic Express

Book Layout ©2022 Ydrate Creates Design
The Poetic Express/Ydrate The Motivator Nelson —1st ed.ISBN
978-0-9860929-1-6

Book Layout ©2022 Ydrate Creates Design
The Poetic Express/ —1st ed.ISBN 978-0-9860929-1-6

Firmly Rooted Optimistic Mind
Meditating Everyday

Taking Opportunities
Years Of Understanding

Volume 1

# The Poetic Express

**By: Ydrate "The Motivator" Nelson**

# The Poetic Guide

## Contents

# II… Essays, Creative Writings & Motivation .......................... 70

*FEED THE HOMELESS*
*MENTOR A CHILD*
*CHERISH THE ELDERLY.*

# I. M.Y. L.I.F.E.

*M*any *Y*ears
*L*iving *I*n *F*aith Everyday.

# My Gift to the World

I f this is the only book I write before I die, then consider this my gift to the world. Initially, I had no intention to write this book. Rather, I started simply writing the things I felt, and as time went on, this book wrote itself. At first, it was just me with a mind full of thoughts, frustrations, and questions, but no fundamental answers or ways to channel my thoughts and emotions. I felt trapped and needed an outlet.

And so, I turned to writing and began to catalog my thoughts. I wrote whatever was on my mind—no matter what. As a result, I created something out of what many would consider nothing: my inner thoughts. Now, I have a physical, tangible, and artistic creation compiled that will stand the test of time.

I found liberation in poetry and creative writing, which guided me on my quest to articulate my vision, define my purpose, and inspire the world. The urgency to publish a book was inspired by the thought of my untimely death and my legacy. If I died today, what would my story be? Who would tell it? What would they say? Would it be the truth as I knew it, or someone else's interpretation of what they thought my truth was? What would I leave behind? Would it even matter that I ever lived?

Like many others, I aspire to live a long, full, and prosperous life. But realistically, only God knows that day and time of expiration. I had to face this reality when I was diagnosed with stage 4 cancer. I wanted to live and believed that I would beat cancer but at the same time, I did not know God's will for my life. I very well could die, taking my dreams, thoughts, and ideas to the grave.

Facing death made me appreciate the privilege of experiencing the beautiful mess I call my life. Each second is a blessing. I recognize that it's crucial for me to make each moment count in a way that builds on the legacy and foundation of my family and ancestors, while glorifying the everlasting kingdom of God Almighty.

My intuitive nature has inspired a spiritual obligation and moral responsibility to plant seeds of love, history, knowledge, and wisdom. In divine timing, some event, act, or deed will have an impact in ways that cannot be calculated or measured by currently defined standards.

These thoughts that I share with you are a reminder that you can achieve any goal you set for yourself. You can make something out of nothing. Your thoughts are valuable assets, and yes, dreams *do* come true. Live your dream today. Make every single day count.

## In your hands is a gift,

## F.R.O.M. M.E. T.O. Y.O.U.

## Volume 1. The Poetic Express.

# *My Prayer for You.*

I pray that God continues to keep,

protect, and bless you, your family, and

everything you touch. I pray that you

prosper in all honorable endeavors. I

pray that you are surrounded by peace,

prosperity, love, and all the goodness of

God's kingdom. I pray that you have

peace, mercy, grace and abundance.

God bless you. I love you. Amen.

# FROM ME TO YOU

To everyone that loves me: I love you back.

To anyone who feels any hatred toward me: I love you, too.

To my supporters: Thank you for your support.

To everyone I have ever hurt: I am sorry.

To my family: I honor and cherish you.

To my friends: Together we stand.

To my foes: Give up. I am protected.

To my children: Learn as much as you can.

To my elders: Teach as much as you can.

To my sisters: Demand the respect of a queen.

To my brothers: We are forever united in the struggle.

To the world: We are all God's children.

To anyone feeling left out or forgotten: Know that God forgets
no one.

# BE THE GREATEST

I am truly grateful for the time you invest with me and my work. Time is life's most valuable resources and I truly appreciate yours. May you continue to be blessed in all honorable endeavors. You are a creation of the Most High. Be the Greatness you were created to be. Don't ever give up on your dreams. You deserve the very Best. BE THE GREATEST.

# My Name is Ydrate

I was born Ydrate Lakeith Nelson. I am often asked about my first name. What does it mean? Where did it come from? How do you pronounce it? Who came up with it? I have never personally met another person who shares my first name in my entire life. I am still looking forward to that opportunity.

My mother told me I was given the name from one of her older sisters, my Aunt who is called Ollie by our family. She named me and several of my cousins. For years people would ask me about my name. What does it mean? Where does it come from? How do you pronounce it? For years I had no real answer for most of those questions outside of what I created and defined myself.

One day I was in little five points in Atlanta, Georgia when I came across a lady who had a name stand. She would type your name into her computer, and it would give the meaning of the name along with additional information depending on the name. She would then print your name and put it in a nice frame. I had already seen this type of set up and was sure they didn't have my name because previous searches reveled nothing.

When I told the lady at the stand that it was no need to search my name because it was nothing there. She then replied, "There has never been a name I haven't found in my data base. If I find your name, you must buy it printed and framed." I agreed and in a second after she typed my name, there it was. The meaning of my name.

- Ydrate gives me self-assurance, independence, and confidence.

- You have depth of mind and the ability to concentrate, and to also follow a line of thought to a logical conclusion.

- Your love of challenging the concepts of others invariably leads you to create your own ideas, and to pioneer new lines of thought.

- Your strong characteristic of individuality qualifies you as a leader.

- You must be independent, and you do not brook interference in any way.

- You do not tolerate interference in your own affairs. This characteristic does not prevent you from interfering in the affairs of others.

- You are usually either telling or showing someone how to do something properly.

- Although you are good-natured and never intend offence, still your blunt, direct, and candid manner of expression strains friendships; your honesty and sincerity earn respect from others.

- You have to be your own boss as it is most difficult for you to submit to directions from others.

- Problems with your health center in head tension, head colds, headaches, and sinus congestion.

# More Than a Book...

This book is more than a book. It is an articulation of my artistic, creative, and emotional freedom. It contains a collection of poems, biographical sketches, memoirs, essays, quotations, and images that have emerged and evolved from my day-to-day life.

Some pieces in this collection are memoirs, memos, thoughts, or unfinished and unpublished fragments of writing that I've intended to finish later. Some are documents that I've developed and refined over time, while many remain the original statement that was committed to paper.

Displaying the essence of a dynamic being, living in a dynamic world, this work is not about one particular subject. This book is a fact-based, creative nonfiction, crossing many genres and subject lines artistically. This work is not limited to one particular experience or event. It is not your typical or traditional published work. This is the manifestation of a dream wrapped up in poetry, prose, and essays.

Writing is a significant part of my life and is a practice I engage in daily for the therapeutic aspect and to chart and track my present and my future. I write to liberate my spirit and save my mind.

Thank you so much for taking the time to engage with my expressions and art. I understand that your time is your most asset, and I am truly blessed that you chose to invest your time with me today. I pray that you continue to be blessed in more ways than you can count. You deserve it. You are a pure Greatness.

*Don't ever stop being who you were created to be. You are truly amazing.*

# Life Lesson

I remember when I thought I was invincible. I never thought much about taking advantage of every moment because I had plenty of time—or at least that's what I thought. In reality, I had procrastination mastered. I didn't think about the consequences of my actions. In fact, looking back, I can identify multiple instances where a different decision or different circumstance would have changed the course of my life.

I could have been incarcerated or dead. In retrospect, I have been extremely blessed and a damn fool. I've gained many things and lost others. I've faced countless challenges and have come out victorious more times than I can count. I have done a lot of things right. And I have done a lot of things wrong. Every event—whether good or bad—has taught me a valuable lesson that had cultivated wisdom and guided my steps as I evolved and grew as a person.

We all go through many experiences that affect our lives in major ways. Many times, we overlook these experiences and brush them off as the nature of life. Although this mentality isn't wrong, it's important to recognize that each experience carries a valuable lesson. Take the opportunity to realize the value of your story and learn from your life lessons. The essence of wisdom can be found in past life experiences. You just have to look.

This is an early family picture taken at my uncle Roberts wedding before I was born back in the 70's. Many of my aunts and uncles are present in this picture. I love to see the legacy of where I came from and the family connection that already existed before I was born. This realization makes me focus on passing along the family traditions and legacy to my children. You can choose your friends, but God blesses you with family. God has truly blessed our family.

# I Love & Cherish My Family.

# They Paved the Way

My great-grandfather, Adam Nelson Senior, born in 1880, was the first generation of born post slavery in my family. Unfortunately, he passed long before I was born; yet without his story, I would not exist. Without his story, I would not have discovered my identify, nor would I have learned more about who I am. Without his sacrifice, I would not be here to tell you both of our stories. In fact, most people wouldn't even know he existed.

Grandpa Adam married my great-grandmother, Mattie May, who was part Cherokee Indian, and also born in 1880. Together they had 9 children and settled in Dublin, Georgia. My great-grandfather made his living as a sharecropper. His pay was meager, but they made the most out of what they had, which was a lot of love. My grandfather lived off the land through agriculture and trading, raising cows, pigs, and chickens in his backyard. He also had a family garden that offered various vegetables to nourish the family.

*I Am because of what they were.*

*Grateful for my Ancestors.*

My great-grandmother oversaw the house and children, and also worked in the fields. Those who knew her referred to her as a wise woman who loved her family dearly. My great-grandparents weren't educated, so their intuition, wisdom, and common sense played a huge roll in their ability to handle adversity and move the family forward. Even without a formal education and comfortable income, they learned to give meaning to life through faith in God and love for one another. They instilled their children with priceless values, such as love, wrath, and respect for God. Through their teachings, they passed on the importance of hard work, commitment, determination, and the value of a dollar to all 9 of their kids. My grandfather, Sammie Nelson, was the youngest of the bunch. I always loved to see how the man I grew up admiring and looking up to was treated like a baby brother by his siblings. Being around my grandfather and his siblings was one of the greatest privaledges of my life.

Mattie May Nelson
1880 - 1962

23

# In the beginning

My mother, Barbara Nelson, felt as though she had made a mistake and let her family down when she found out she was going to be a teen mother. She cried when my grandmother walked in the room and asked her what was wrong. When my mother finally confided in her, my grandmother lovingly responded with, "Don't worry about it. This Baby is a blessing. Sometimes God turns the things that seem bad into good. Don't worry."

From the time I was born until the day I graduated from high school, I never experienced a need that went unmet. My mother, her 10 sisters and brothers, and my grandparents pitched in to ensure I had everything I needed. My grandparents treated me like their very own, and my aunts and uncles treated me like their little brother or son.

From the time I was born all the way until I could take care of myself, I had my family's support. Since so many people invested in me, I knew I needed to return the favor by investing in and blessing others to keep the cycle alive. I will never forget what my family has done for me, nor will I neglect the opportunity to help other people who truly need it. Family is far more precious than all the money and material possessions in the world. We must cherish them as our greatest possession.

# *Barbara Nelson*

The year is 1977 and 18 year old Barbara Nelson is about to be the mother of a baby boy. Her life will be changed forever. I am grateful for her sacrifice. I love you mother.

# My Humble Beginnings

As a child growing up in Dublin, Georgia, we lived on a dirt road in a little white house. My mother and I, along with a few other family members, lived at my grandparent's house.

Looking back, this period of time brought me some of the best days. There were 6 rooms in total: 3 bedrooms, a kitchen, a living room, and a family room. The house didn't have a foundation, and it was supported by bricks that elevated it a few feet off the ground. In the early years, we didn't even have a bathroom. I can still remember the day we finally installed indoor plumbing. Still, my grandfather opted to use our backyard outhouse.

In this small house with shingle siding and a tin roof lived my grandparents, my two aunts, my two uncles, my young cousin, Latansey, and my mother. I was blessed to have so many people in one household to teach, lead, and guide me. At the time, it often felt difficult and frustrating because there were so many people waiting to tell me what to do. But through these negative emotions, my grandmother used to always say, "Baby, one day you will be your own man. You will be able to do whatever you want to, but until that day, you need to listen to and respect what grown folks tell you." It was hard to understand then, but now I get it.

Living with my grandparents was one of my life's most rewarding experiences. They taught me to be a leader and they taught me the true value of family. These are gifts of life that I will carry and pass on to my children in hopes that the values I learned will inspire their life the way they inspired mine.

Now, I am blessed with an amazing opportunity to do something great for my family. Without the sacrifice of those who came before me, I would not have this opportunity. I am humbled and grateful to continue my ancestors' tradition and legacy. I often wonder what my great-grandparents would think of the opportunity that me and my kids have today. We can't let them down.

We are all born with the same potential to do something great. Many of us are less fortunate than others, but that doesn't take away from our potential to do all that we desire. Whether you're from a rich family or a poor one, don't let anyone devalue the wealth of your being. What did the lifestyle you lived growing up teach you?

# Do You Believe?

I was born in a small, mid-Georgia town in Dublin, located 130 miles southeast of Atlanta, and about 120 miles northwest of Savannah—almost perfectly centered between the two cities. We're a close nit community. Everyone either knows you or knows a member of your immediate family.

Growing up, our town only had three public high schools and one private school. Even now, we don't have many big industries driving the economy. Instead, we have a perfect blend of community support that provide all citizens with enough work to support their families. No matter where I go, who I meet, or where I live, I will always love Dublin, Georgia, my hometown.

Reflecting on this aspect of my life, I learned that no matter where you're from, you have the potential to go anywhere you can dream of. Be proud of where you are from and take pride in your community. There is no place like home.

*No matter where you go, never forget where you are from. There is no place like home.*

I love and appreciate you.

# Life on the farm

My grandfather was an agricultural master, and he grew the majority of the food we ate, including corn, peas, collard greens, peppers, onions, tomatoes, watermelon, cantaloupe, melons, and spices—to name a few. We had a fig tree that we used to make preserves and a peach tree that we used to make cobbler. He grew sugarcane, which we used to make syrup once a year. We even slaughtered our own cows, pigs, deer, rabbit, skirl, possums, raccoons, and chickens.

My grandfather took some of the surplus from the garden to the local markets and traded them for other meats and foods that we didn't have. Even though we didn't have a lot of money, we never went hungry. My grandfather would gather the food and my grandmother would prepare it. They were the perfect team.

I often still dream of living just one more day on the farm. It was all so simple.

Growing up watching my grandfather the farmer, I learned that it's not about what you want, but rather what you need. I learned how to use and maximize the resources around me. And as a result, I never experienced hunger for a single day, regardless of how much money I had in my pocket.

My grandmother taught me how to take charge. She was never shy about giving commands that got the job done. She was a hard worker, and often led by example. I also developed my culinary skills and passion for cooking from watching my grandmother excel in the kitchen. She used creativity and innovation to engineer many meals that nourished both our stomachs and our souls.

This is one of the few pictures I have of my Grandparents house. I was raised in this house and learned many life lessons under the tin roof of this house. Most of my firsts in life took place in this house located on a dusty dirt road right outside the city limits of Dublin, GA.

I remember at one point, there was 9 people living in this house. We never considered ourselves or family as poor because he never lacked for anything. We always had the basics of life, food, clothing and shelter.

No matter how far I go, what I do or how I do it, there will always be a part of the lesson I leaned from this 6-room house in my heart. The house has been torn down, but the memories will always build me up. I'm from the DUB.

# Killing of the Chickens

I particularly remember the killing of the chickens. We all played a part. My grandfather would retrieve the best chicken while one of my uncles boiled the water for defeathering. My grandmother would ring the chicken's neck, and I would round up newspaper to burn the feathers and retrieve the chicken afterward.

Since my grandparents' house was elevated off the ground with bricks, the chickens often flopped to their death, nearly bouncing under the house. My grandmother would warn, "Boy, if you let that chicken go under the house, you're going to get him." In fear of what was living under there, I did my best to keep the chicken from flopping under. It always fascinated me to see an animal that was walking around our yard earlier that day sitting on my plate that following night.

I take for granted the meaning of true home cooked meals and home-grown food as I rush from drive-thru to drive-thru in search of a anything to quickly satisfy my hunger. What I was lacking, however, was food that also satisfied my soul.

*My life experiences made me who I am.*

This picture is one of the most important pictures in the history of my family. I was barely a year old and that me in my Grandfather's lap. My entire family embraced me from the time I was born to the present day. I was blessed with 6 uncles, 4 aunts, mother and grandparents. I had all my first cousins as my first friends and partners in crime.

I will forever be wealthy not because of money but because of the family connection that is more valuable than all the money in the world. I truly love and appreciate my family. Without them, I would not be the person I am today.

# My First Heroes

My grandfather tended to the property that was adjacent to our land. We only had about an acre or so, but that property was about 30. We had full access to it and rarely saw the owner. There were about 20 cows and 5 horses, and my grandfather was responsible for feeding the animals, mowing the fields, and maintaining the property. Each day, he'd ensure they all had water and food and would herd the animals from field to field. I often tagged along because I was interested in understanding how just one man could be responsible for so much. He was my hero to me and there was nothing better than watching my hero in action.

On that property was a pond. My grandmother loved to fish, and we would often take a short walk up the dirt road to the bank of the pond. After my grandfather and I gathered worms for bait, we'd sit on the bank for hours, patiently waiting for the fish to fall into our traps. Out of boredom, I'd sometimes skip rocks accords the water, until my grandmother ordered me stop scaring away the fish. It was no secret what would be for supper that night.

Fishing taught me incredible patience. I learned how to make something out of nothing, and I learned that we all have a role to play in accomplishing the tasks we set out to accomplish.

I heard my grandfather say countless times, "It's better to have it and not need it than to need it and not have it."

I could not see it when I was younger but all of those life lessons and quotes, I learned from my Grandparents would be the guide for my life. I am grateful for my first true Heroes.

My Grandparents Sammy and Marion Nelson. Most people referred to them as Fat and Sister Nelson. They made me into the person I am today. I learned most of the lessons in life from them. I cherish their legacy and work to protect and expand it daily. There is no way I could have been blessed with better Grandparents. They were my first true heroes.

My Grandparents Roosevelt and Clara Thomas. I still remember Grandma Clara would come to Southwest Elementary to see me when I was in kindergarten. She would give me peppermints and a few quarters as we walked around the hallways. She was always, kind and classy. My Grandfather Roosevelt Thomas was known for his legendary strength. I hear stories about his ability and tenacity reinforces the strength I see in myself and my children.

A collection of photos from Sammy "Fat" Nelson including one sitting on the front porch enjoying the afternoon with his prized garden over his shoulder. That garden provided food for 3 generations when I was growing up. My Grandmother would always say, "this is some of the best food you will ever eat." I used to beg to differ, now I completely agree. I wish I could have one more meal from my grandfather's garden and my grandmother's kitchen.

My Big Cousin Bonita was the coolest person in our family when I was growing up. She took us to the park on the southside, to the skating rink and trips to Atlanta. From the time I can remember to the present day she has always had my back. This is a picture of us going back over 40 years. I am grateful for the role she has played and continues to play to this day. I love you Cuzzo.

My cousin **Sanyo** was my first friend I can recall in life. She was like my big sister, and I was her little genie pig. She would have me on all types of adventures and missions. When she moved, I moved. When she got her driver's license, it was like I got mine as well. She is 2 years older and taught me about style and swag. I had none and she had it all. I appreciate the genuine love and mentorship. My cousin made me a better more confident pre and teenager. That confidence carried over into my life.

*Ydrate*
*Lakeith*
*Nelson*

Top Left - 1986 Picture Day at Southwest Laurens Elementary. I can still hear my mother asking me why I had that smile on my face. My attempt at a smile didn't work out. I now see my 6-year-old doing the same thing.

Middle - Ydrate Nelson (1980). In this picture, I was about 3 years old. I now see this same face in my 3-year-old sons. That lets me know I must set the right example because they are walking in and following my footsteps.

Bottom Left - This is me back in 1978. A young Ydrate Lakeith Nelson before I could walk or talk. I had no idea or consciousness about the adventure's life would bring my way. I have truly been blessed.

Top Right – 1979 – I still this little ball was my favorite for years. I still remember the day I lost it under my grandparents' house. I don't know what it was with me and that ball, but I had it for year, and it is in my memory for life

Bottom Right - 1987 Rentz Giants. I will never forget this era in my life. It was the first time I was ever on a team and my uncle Nathaniel Nelson was a coach. I learned lessons about teamwork and racism that year that I never forgot. One of my teammates who I went to battle with on the field was the first person to ever call me a nigger. I was hurt at the time, but I consider that experience a blessing today. It was the first but not the last time I would face racism. It taught me a lot about the world we live in and helped prepare me for the journey ahead. I am grateful for this season on and off the field.

# My First Heart Break

It was June 13, 1995, in Dublin, GA. I was supposed to work a summer job assembling light fixtures my aunt helped me get at the plant that employed her. However, one day, I decided to skip work so I could instead attend summer workouts for football; I couldn't miss the first game of the year—after all, it was my senior year.

I was at my grandparents' house next door when the time I would normally leave for work approached. My grandmother urged me to head to work so as not to be late, so I told her I was instead planning on attending football practice. She responded, "Boy, you better take your behind to work. Those people trusted you enough to give you a job. When somebody gives you a chance, you do all you can. Leave

before you're late." I agreed, kissed her, and told her I'd see her the next dayI didn't go to work that day. I went to football practice.

Since my mom and sisters lived next door to my grandparents, when I returned home that night, I turned my music and head lights off so my grandmother wouldn't notice that I returned home early. I made it in the house unseen, took a shower, and laid across my mother's California-king-sized bed.   I had just dialed a friend when I heard a violent knock at the door. I jumped and ran to see what the commotion was about.

My mother and I met at the back door greeting my grandfather who was out of breath. "Something's wrong with your Ma. I don t know if she's dead or what," he said. I had never seen that look on his face, and so, I knew it had to be serious. My mother and I ran the 20-yards to my grandparents' house. When we entered the room, my grandmother was lying on her back across the bed, completely unresponsive. My mother went to her side to revive her and I called for help.

Within minutes, my aunts, uncle, and a host of cousins had arrived. Shortly after the paramedics made it, I felt hope. I knew they would revive her, get her to the hospital, and all would be okay. I knew they would bring her back.

But I was wrong. A blanket of sadness and gloom enveloped the home and everyone inside. My grandmother was pronounced dead. My reality shifted in that moment, and shock overcame me. I had spent the greater part of my life under her watchful eye and she was resting in peace before me—breathless and motionless. Lifeless.

I walked outside and stood in the yard, confused, when a set of head lights came around the corner. It was the black Hurst from *Dudley's Funeral Home*. They pulled right up to the back door to carry my grandmother away for the last time. I watched as they rolled her lifeless body out of the house and into the car, slamming the doors shut behind her. Then, the black Cadillac backed out of the yard and disappeared down the dark, dusty dirt road. I watched the taillights vanish in the night along with a piece of my heart. Panic set in as so many questions flooded my head. *What just happened? What do we do next?* Our lives were changed forever.

Despite the countless lessons I learned from my grandmother, the day she passed taught me something invaluable. The last conversation we ever had was about the importance of being responsible and going to work. To this day, I still hear those final words echoing in my mind, "When somebody gives you a chance, you do all you can."

This picture was taken the day after my Grandmother passed away. I was the saddest I had even been in life. My heart was broken into a 1,000 pieces. I became a different person on this day. My life has never been the same. My grandfather was devasted, but he handled the lost with such dignity and grace. He inspired me to face and deal with adversity in a graceful way.

# Glad he missed

(October 1995) It was senior year and my team had just won our varsity football game. I was particularly excited because I had played well. We held a school dance afterward, and I danced with about every girl in the building.

At the end of the night, I went out to my car when two of my friends informed me that some guys from another school were going to jump me for dancing with one of their girlfriends. I wasn't really concerned, and so I dismissed the warning. My young cousin and a couple of my friends jumped into the truck, and we went to McDonald's—the typical hang-out spot after all the high school sports games. Shortly after I arrived, a car with five young boys pulled up and parked across from me.

My friends pointed them out as the guys who wanted to fight me. They told me to approach them—our town was small and we'd eventually cross paths. And so, I walked into the middle of the parking lot between my vehicle and theirs. "What's the problem?" I asked. They all either dropped their heads or looked the other way. I turned around and looked to my friends who beckoned for me to return where we were posted. As I walked away, one of the guys opened fire. He barely missed me but hit the vehicle I was driving. I heard the gunshot and the deafening *clink* as the bullet pierced the side of the truck. A couple inches to one side and better aim, my life would have been a lot different—or simply over.

Life is incredibly precious and full of close calls. Many situations we face could change the course of our lives. We must consider all the small blessings that we've been given and be grateful for where we are. A second or an inch could be the difference between life and death. I am blessed to be alive.

---

(1991) My 8<sup>th</sup> grade year I was the MVP of my team and delivered my first public speech ever. We also lost every game that year. Even though we didn't win on the scoreboard I remember pushing through adversity to complete the season with my team. I also remember enjoying the process with my team. I learned that winning is not always about the scoreboard

My senior class voted me Best All Around. I was really honored because many of them didn't know the adversity I was facing during that year. This year taught me how to deal with adversity continue to press forward. It laid the foundation for the rest of my life. I am truly grateful I made it out and now my mission is to guide and inspire others to do the same.

.

(Class of 1996) After playing in a Raider uniform for 6 years, my senior year came and went by so quick. It was over but the memories from the process are with me forever. We never won a state championship, but we played until the final horn. Our team motto was, "Work Hard, Get Better". That has been a lesson that I carry for life. I am forever grateful for my athletic experience and Raider Nation. Ydrate Nelson #50

**Best All Around**

"Katasha Johnson could not be placed in one category to describe what a wonderful person she is. She is a combination of all the other superlatives in one." Y'drate Nelson

"Y'drate Nelson is a down to earth person. He's athletic, gets along with everyone, dresses nice, make good grades, and talks to everybody. There are a lot of good things to say about him, but best all around sums it up." Katasha Johnson

# Welcome to Chic Fil A

At the end of 1995, leading into 1996, the football season was over. It was time for me to find a job and get to work. Since I was on track to graduate, I signed up for a class that would allow me to leave for the second half of the school day and go to work. All I needed was a job and I would be able to leave school early each day and go to work.

Back then, we did not have a home computer, so I searched the local newspaper for jobs. I was led to an ad for a brand-new Chic Fil A that was being built in my hometown of Dublin, Georgia. I went and filled out the application. The store was still being built at the time and the store had not opened. A few days later I was interviewing for the job. I was one of the first people hired by my new mentor Dave Roberts.

This job was very important to me because it was the first time, I had the opportunity to put to action the last lesson my grandmother taught me on the day she passed away. I was eager to get to work, prove my worth, and honor my grandmother's legacy. I took my position very seriously from the very first day. I was all in on proving my worth and applying what Grandma taught me.

Ready to get to work, I was there from day one to help assemble and install all the shelves. I was also there when the final equipment arrived. I was there when the first truck pulled up to deliver food. I still remember unloading the boxes of chicken and the fries. I remember the first time we cooked a chicken and assembled a sandwich. I learned how to do every single job in the entire building. From running the cash register to cooking all the food, I was all in on my job.

Each day during the second semester, I would leave after lunch and go straight to work. Being able leave school early daily allowed me to get full time hours. It wasn't long before I was promoted to crew leader. I worked and gave Dave and Chic Fil A all I had because I could not get the last conversation with my grandmother out of my head. On top of that, I was living with my grandfather and had to wake up and go to sleep in the house that my grandmother passed away in. I thought about her every time I clocked in.

As soon as I graduated from high school, I was promoted to a store manager. Dave Roberts trusted me with his entire store. There would be times when I would close at night and then be there to open the store the next day. I would count all the money, make deposits, and even allowed to conduct interviews at the age of 18. I was proud of my job and honored that the owner Dave, trusted me so much. It was the most responsibility I had ever been given and it was an honor.

I worked all summer and saved as much as I could. I was on the fence about what to do with my future and I pondered my options. That fall, I made the decision to leave Dublin, GA to attend college in Valdosta, GA. I still remember the day I clocked out for the last time. It was bittersweet. I was saying goodbye to my current job but hello to my future.

When I left Dublin, I decided to transfer my job because they had a Chic Fil A in the city I was moving to. When I got to Valdosta, I still had my manger shirts and uniform from my time at the store in my hometown. I was quickly humbled. The store was in the mall where all the college students shopped. Instead of picking up with my managerial position, I was put on fries and told that I would have to start at the bottom as a new employee and work my way to the top. There was a long line of tenured people in from of me and my experience bared no weight. I had to relinquish my manger shirt, return to my duty as the fry guy.

I would often work the register and took orders from my college friends and classmates. This was a long way from where I was when I left Dublin. It was a humbling experience to go from management to not having your experience respected or count with the same company. I worked there for about a year and left due to limited hours.

The first job I applied for beyond Chic Fil A was for a local gas station chain in Valdosta. The first person I put as a reference was my old manager at Chic Fil A, Dave Roberts. The hiring manger contacted Dave. After their conversation, the hiring manager called me back the same day to offer me the job. He said that his decision was based on the conversation he had with Dave. He said he was advised to hire and promote me as soon as possible.

That job secured me financially for a few years while in college. Even though I was working outside of the Chi Fil A company, I was still benefiting from the family I made while I was there. I am and will be forever grateful for Dave Roberts and the Chic Fil A family for the role they played in my life.

As a 20 year old college student in 1998 at Valdosta State University, I made the decision to become a member of Alpha Phi Alpha Fraternity Inc. This picture was taken on the night we revealed our identity to the student body on our campus. This was one of the most memorable nights of my life

# Tell Your Story

Millions of people wish they could write or publish a book, start a business, or go back to school. But a wish is just a goal without a plan. Without a plan, it's impossible to transforms wishes into reality. We are all authors, and the unique book of each of our lives is writing itself every second of every day. We are all a culmination of our individual stories, events, and experiences.

Most of us have faced extreme situations that have changed the course of our lives. We have all felt the joy of the highest high, and the agony of the lowest low. We all have accomplishments that we cherish, and obstacles that taught us valuable life lessons.

We all have a story, so don't be afraid to share yours. Somebody out there needs to hear what you have to say. Whether or not you write it down, you live your life story every day. Realize the value of your story and never underestimate its power.

*I pray God continues to Bless You and Your Family. You are a Blessing to the World. I appreciate you.*

(2000) While in college I had a chance to visit my father in Hawaii with my younger brother DJ. This is the first picture we ever took together in life. We had just stepped off the plane at the Honolulu Airport. This was the farthest I had ever been away from Georgia and this trip changed my life forever. I never saw life the same.

# Fallen Legend

(2004) I got a call from my cousin one day. When I answered, he said, "He

Ydrate, you heard about Granddad?" I said I hadn't, and before he could even respond, my eyes started to fill with tears as my heartbeat rapidly accelerated. "He's really sick and they said he might not make it through the night." In that moment, I was overcome with emotion once more.

He survived the night, but he was in extreme pain. When I walked in the room the next day to visit him, he was asleep. But still, he kept moaning and groaning as the pain from the cancer was eating him alive. I didn't want to wake him, so I just sat there instead. About an hour or so passed and he finally awoke. "Don't you come in my room again without waking me up," he warned.

To see the first man I had ever looked up to and admired in excruciating pain caused me incredible grief. I couldn't bear seeing him hurt. I asked the nurse if there was anything they could do to help make him more comfortable, but there wasn't.

For the next few days, I hung around the hospital and watched my grandfather grow weaker and weaker by the day. The pain that I saw him endure was a deep burden on my soul. I felt that he didn't deserve it and I would have done anything to just ease his suffering. But unfortunately, things only got worse. On one Sunday afternoon, with my entire family at the hospital, the nurse informed us that his time was nearing. I stood by his side, watched him breathe, and couldn't blink, fearing I'd miss his last breath.

Then, he took one deep breath and exhaled for the last time. His chest never rose again. I removed the tube from his nose, wiped his mouth, grabbed him by his hand, and prayed.

A few minutes later, the nurse pronounced him dead. I thought I would be overcome by grief and emotional pain, but what I felt surprised me. Relief washed over me. I was proud of who my grandfather was and I knew he no longer had to worry, suffer, or feel any pain. I was sad because I knew I'd miss him in this life, but I also knew that the lessons he taught me, and my family would live on.

As I watched my grandfather take his last breath, I found peace in death I had never before experienced or thought possible. In that moment, I looked around the hospital room and saw his 11 kids, 30 grandkids, and several great grandkids. His work on earth was well done and there was nothing left for him to accomplish. He lived a full and inspirational life. He will forever be immortalized to me and is my example of what a real man is and should be.

# Fade to Black

(2005) I was on the phone with my dear friend Vonda as her brother, Chris, one of my closet friends, pulled into his driveway. He was ambushed by some men posted outside of his home. Vonda heard gunshots and ran outside, only to see a vehicle fleeing the scene and her brother lying on the street. "Please, somebody help me! My brother's been shot," she screamed. Within minutes, a few of my friends and I arrived at the scene just as the police arrived. They stopped us before we could get any closer.

From where we were parked, I saw the exhaust escaping from the tail pipe of Chris' Platinum colored Jaguar as his motor ran. I slowly walked around the back of the vehicle I was in and saw a glimpse of my friend's body lying next to his car. The bullet shattered his windshield as the music he was listening to played on in the background. My heart was beating through my chest as confusion set in. I stared at my friend's body as if he would get up any second, brush himself off, and walk inside his childhood home. He never moved. On July 25, 2005, one of my closest friends, Christopher Wright, was murdered.

I stood and watched the entire investigation unfold for over three hours. I heard the conversation as the police, detectives, and crime investigator surveyed the murder scene. I watched every move that was made, as if their actions would change what had already been done. An officer approached my friends and I and told us we couldn't watch. And so, I moved a few meters away and stood behind a tree as one man grabbed him by his feet and another grabbed him by his hands, placing his body in a black bag.

As they moved my friend from the street to the back of a coroner's white van, slamming the doors behind them and driving way, I felt a piece of my heart drive away with them.

We had an ambitious conversation about big plans we had for the future the day before he died. He said, "Dog, I got you. I'm a fan and a supporter. I've always believed in you. I'm telling you, just keep grinding. It's going to happen." I would have never expected  that those words would be among the last I'd ever hear from him.

A week later, I found myself at his funeral in his hometown of Valdosta, GA. As I heard the pastor speak about Chris' life, I thought reflected on my own and thought about how I wanted to be represented in death. My life was forever changed in that moment, as my purpose was being redefined before my eyes.

The death of Chris Wright is one of the single most influential and motivational lessons in my life. I never felt pain like the pain I felt that day. I couldn't fathom the emotional roller coaster I was on when he passed. I fell into a deep depression and found every possible way to blame myself for something that was far beyond my control. It was one of my lowest points in life. I was unemployed, broke, and had just lost a dear friend. I was lost and felt sorry for myself. I remember praying to God and asking for help: "God, please help me. I don't know what to do and I don't want to feel like this anymore." From that day on, I regained control of my life again. I prayed for guidance every day and gradually started to work my way up from one of my lowest points to a strong mentality.

Not a day has passed where I don't think of Chris. When I looked at his pictures, I often cried and felt incredible pain in my chest as I tried to process the incident. At times, I would even dial his number and listen to his voicemail. Then, one day, all the hurt I felt was gone. Just like that, the sadness I felt disappear. Today, when I look at his pictures, I no longer suffer. Instead, I feel a sense of pride and security. I know I can still go to him for advice in the spiritual realm. He is there, watching above me, and I will forever miss his presence in the physical world.

I learned that you may never truly overcome some things in life, and so, you must learn to live with them and live through them.

Chris Wright (August 24, 1972 – July 31, 2005) was a former award-winning Canadian Football League kick returner and Grey Cup champion.

Wright played college football at Georgia Southern. His first year as a professional was successful, for as kick returner with the Baltimore Stallions he scored 3 touchdowns on punt returns and added an 82-yard punt return for a touchdown in their Grey Cup victory. This won him the Frank M. Gibson Trophy as best rookie in the CFL Southern Conference, and an all-star selection.

He moved north to Canada with the Stallions when they relocated and became the revived Montreal Alouettes. He missed the entire 1996 season due to injury, but had an impressive 1997 campaign, with 2 punt return touchdowns. He was released after the 1998 season, but resurfaced in 2002 with the BC Lions, where he played 7 games. Chris Wright was murdered in a shooting in Atlanta on July 31, 2005.

From 2003 to 2005, I was still hungry for success and worked towards my goals daily of being successful in the music business. I made a ton of mistakes and learned a lot during this phase. Following my trip to Hawaii, I literally went 9 years without a haircut. I was locked in. This picture was taken by legendary director Crystal "Clear" Roberson

# I am On a Mission

I am on a mission, and I am here to do my part. I choose to use my God-given abilities of creation, expression, and a positive attitude to educate, motivate, and inspire a lifestyle of creativity, harmony, love, prosperity, and self-expression.

I work to encourage you to live your dream. I developed my skillsets in hopes that my efforts would inspire you to do the same. I will continue on my journey to bridge the gap between the past, present, and future generations to come.

Note that my goal is not to convince you to be like me or do what I do. We all define greatness based on standards set from within that can't be scaled or measured, and my goal is to encourage you to determine what the *best you* looks like, and work toward achieving it every day.

I realized that no relationship, business, or plan would stand the test of time, unless built on truth, justice, and integrity. As long as the creator blesses me with life in the physical realm and in spirit, I will strive to use my blessing to bless others, and to also encourage you to do the same. When the Highest graduates us to the next level of eternal prosperity, we will let the work we have done speak for us, and also allow the everlasting spirit to preserve our life.

We are on a mission, and I am just doing my part. What is your mission?

*No matter where you are from, you have the potential to go anywhere you dream of. Keep you focus, on your mission.*

# Live From The PHX

(March 2008) After living in Georgia for over 30 years, I made the decision to relocate to Phoenix, Arizona where my father lived. I left most of my family and friends in the south and I ventured out west for new adventures. I was blessed to be working a company that allowed me to transfer my job and it was a smooth transition.

I didn't plan on staying out west because I loved Atlanta and the state of Georgia but the opportunity for advancement with the company I was working for lead me to stay much longer. I was promoted to a management position with  the agreement I would stay for a year. I left that company many years ago but I never left Phoenix.

When I first moved to Phoenix everything was different from what I saw my entire life. There was nothing that resembled my previous life. The air, sky, topography, demographics, landscape all different.

Growing up in Georgia, grass, trees and green landscape dominate your view. In Phoenix, everything was brown, no grass and very few natural trees. Instead of the pine trees that dominated Georgia, I would see cactus mixed with palm trees. Seeing different surrounding inspired different thoughts.

While living in Arizona, I was able to establish myself outside the comfort of my familiar environment. I left the comforts of certainty and ventured into the unknow. The decision to move across the country was one of the best of my life.

Since relocating to Arizona, I have received several community recognitions including, Mitch Akin Mentor of the Year, Bank of America Local Hero Award recipient, PALS Mentor of the Year, 10 time award winning speaker, The Difference Maker Award Winner and Teacher of The Year.

My life has been blessed and the foundation for elevation has been established. I have been able to grow in ways that I could not while living in Georgia. While I did have some adversity along the way, it was a necessary part of the process. I was able to use everything as a learning opportunity and grow into a better person.

No matter what I do or where I go, there will always be love and respect for the role living in Arizona played in my development.

# I Met A Queen

I was living in Phoenix for a little over a year when one of my friends from Georgia came out to visit. Being a good host, I took him to a local spot to hang out. Little did I know, I would meet a lady that would change my life forever.

I was approached by a lady who had an interest in my visiting friend. As a 'prize' she offered me a cupcake. Little did I know, the cupcake would change the direction of my life. I was approached by a lady who questioned me about eating her red velvet cupcake. I referred to her friend that gave me permission.

I introduced myself and found out the owner of the red velvet was celebrating her birthday. She was very attractive in her purple  birthday outfit, and I was interested in helping her celebrate. From that moment, we have been connected. We have not missed celebrating a birthday together since then. We got married on her birthday a few years later and went on to have 4 kids.

Never did I think a chance encounter would impact my life on so many levels. I often look at my kids and think, what would my life be like if I would have opted to take my visiting friend to a different spot to entertain. My reality would be different. I am grateful that the universal order and divine timing led me to my queen.

# Nothing to Lose

Publishing a book was one of the scariest experiences of my life. I am taking something from my heart and soul, giving it to the universe, and allowing the world to judge me based on it. Many of my insecurities found their way to the forefront of my mind. I asked myself, "What if I make a mistake or mess up? Why am I really publishing this book, and what do I hope to achieve?"

I felt vulnerable for exposing the personal aspects of my life. I thought, "Why would anyone even want to read this? What if they don't like it or think I am crazy? What if I make a fool of myself?" Over the course of time, many thoughts made me question myself, my motive, and my ability.

One day, I had a realization. It dawned on me that I was worrying about the inevitable. All those thoughts didn't matter. Certainly, there would be millions of people who won't buy my book, support me in any way, or even care to learn my name. Inevitably, there are many who will think I am crazy. At some point in this process, I will probably make a fool of myself. Once I recognize this and came to terms with it, I was left with one last question: "What do I have to lose?"

I decided to face my fears and go for it. I held onto faith and let God work it out. Going forward, I will accept the challenges and criticisms that come my way. I will not get overly consumed by what other people think. I will focus on manifesting the vision God has put in my heart. I have nothing to lose.

Just go for it. Whatever *it* is. Don't hold yourself back. Give yourself the permission you need to achieve all the things you want to achieve.

It is time to live your best life. You are blessed to be here, and it is time to maximize your potential. Don't make excuses, only make plays. You have nothing to lose.

# Keep the Faith

I started with nothing. I had no money, no car, no job, lost the love of my life, and was in debt when I wrote the first words of this book. It started off entirely for myself because I couldn't see the peak of the mountains that stood before me when I was deep in the valley.

By the grace of God and God alone, I made it through. I know it was God because I gave up on myself. But in my darkest hour, I prayed to God for help. Even when I lost faith in myself and lost the clarity of my vision, I had faith that God would get me through, and He did.

Honestly speaking, I didn't know how I would get to where I wanted to be, but I knew I would get there. I reminded myself that it wasn't about falling, but rather about getting up and reaching for support when needed. I knew that if I lost focus and faith in my vision, I would need to find some universal force to guide me. In my case, this was God. And so, I believed, and I kept my faith.

God gave each of us an individual purpose. Seek guidance to clarify your purpose. Amid all the confusion, maintain your vision. We all must get in touch with who we are to ensure we are truly living the life God intends for us to live. Just keep your faith.

Always keep the faith and Believe in yourself.

You can do anything you put your mind too.

Keep the faith and make it happen

# II... Essays, Creative Writings & Motivation

Writing became my therapy and my plan for liberation. When I was in the 5th grade I heard Zig Zigler speaking on a cassette tape in English class. It was the first time I heard or paid attention to someone who was speaking with such an inspirational tone. It made me feel way inside. I was truly inspired. I can still remember thinking to myself, man I would love to do that and make people feel that way.

It was not until I saw Les Brown that I saw the reality for myself. I saw a video him speaking at the Georgia dome in front of tens of thousands of people. That is when I knew. This is it. This is what I want for my life. I didn't know exactly how to make it happen, but I knew that motivating and inspiring was attached to my life calling.

During my 20's, I had a huge focus on creating positive music. I didn't focus on the speaking business because I was locked in on the music business. Most of my friends and affiliates were all working towards music business success. As I grew beyond my 20's the focused moved from the music, back to the speaking, teaching and motivating.

Over the years of creating, I wrote thousands of words in search of my voice. Some of the pieces were designed to be speeches, others simple thoughts, essays, and creative writing. One day I was looking through my notes and came across a collection of different material I collected over the years. Many other documents, I had already lost to misplaced notebooks and crashed computers.

I thought to myself, what are you going to do with these writings? I decided to package them up and give them to the world.

When that day of my inevitable departure from this human experience comes, I will have something to leave behind that reflects my existence. Some of these thoughts developed into more refined documents while others remained in the same simple thought that created them.

The delivery modality has changed over the years but the desire to motivate and inspire has remained. Now I am sharing with you some of my pure thoughts in hopes that something will inspire you to BE THE GREATEST version of yourself.

This is for YOU...You are loved and appreciated. You are a valuable asset to this world and I thank God for you. You were created to be GREAT and I pray peace and prosperity follow you and your family. God Bless You. #DoUBelieve #BETHEGREATEST

www.YdrateNelson.com

# Artistic Expression

Living and working in a politically charged, corporate world, I often found myself compromising my feelings and silencing my voice. Whether the topic is race, politics, or religion, I often contained my thoughts to a very selective group of ears. I have stood on stages and in meetings in suit and tie, smiling and saying what I was directed to say to the audience, while suppressing the true contents of my heart.

I have trodden very lightly, doing the best I can to avoid stepping on any toes, or offending others. I have held back things I should have screamed. I was a prisoner of myself, confined to the limits of my own consciousness. I have compromised the integrity of my truth. And so, I realized I needed an outlet.

Creative writing and poetry allow me to get it all out. I can say everything that I want to say in a way that liberates me, without alienating others. I can express the desires of my heart. I can vent and rant about the unjust world. I can express love, hate, disappointment, and joy. I can be creative and compose something that has never existed.

# Come as you are...

It does not matter who you are, how much you have or don't have, your race, skin color, ethnicity, education, gender, location, birthplace, likes, dislikes, age, hair color and/or texture, sex, sexual preference, disability, or your religion. We are united on more fronts than we acknowledge. Rather than focusing on our differences, let's take a closer look at what makes us alike. Let's look at the things that bring us together, instead of the distinctions that tear us apart.

We all need oxygen and water to live. We all have feelings, emotions, and desires. We all want to provide for our families and live prosperous lives. We all live under the same sun, and we see the reflection of the same moon. We can no longer be segregated by our differences. We must instead build on the uniting factors that bring us together.

Amid all our differences that separate us, there is a universal order that applies to every living species and brings us all together: love— the foundation of life. Even if we

BE THE GREATEST.

Hard times and adversity are part of life but don't forget to smile and appreciate it all. #DoUBelieve #BETHEGREATEST

www.YdrateNelson.com

manage to acquire all the heights of success, including iconic status and material riches, without love, we have nothing. Love is biblical, global, and universal in its reach.

I often imagine a world filled with love and recognize that although I can't change the people around me, forcing them to adhere to my perspective, I *can* control my own actions. In a constant effort to eliminate hatred, envy, jealousy, spite, and selfishness toward others, I will deploy love above all, and encourage those around me to do the same.

In a world that is full of conflict and war—both foreign and domestic—I will do a service to humanity by putting aside any differences, and I'll unite in the spirit of love as we work to make the world as we know it a better place. I know that together, our dreams will become opportunities, and the ideas we have will become portraits on the wall for the world to see all that we accomplished.

# Be proud of where you are from,

# and take pride in your community.

# Don't Get Boxed In

Too often, I have allowed other people to limit me, my thinking, and my opportunities by telling me I could not succeed, thus leading me to fear failure and the ridicule that comes along with it. They told me something wasn't possible, and silly me, for years, I believed them.

But then, I realized I was my own person, and no one could define me or the things I was capable of. From that point onward, I refused to allow the limitations that others placed on themselves to be placed on me.

I decided to define myself based on who I knew I was, opposed to who others thought I was. I destroyed the box.

Don't allow others to put limitations on your life. Know your own value and self-worth. Define your own greatness, and don't get boxed in.

# Qualify Yourself

Many people have asked me, "What qualifies you to be an author?"

I am no better or different than anybody else. I'm not from a financially rich family with a number of assets. I am not from a large city with influential friends.

I did not attend a highly accredited university and obtain a prestigious degree. I am not famous for anything I have accomplished. I am just an average person, living an average life, with a big dream. I am just like you.

The qualifications I have to write this book are the same qualifications you have to achieve whatever your dreams might be. I qualify myself, and you I urge you to do the same.

One day, my physical body will be gone, but my words, thoughts, and feelings will stand forever. The life I live qualifies me to be anything God has put in my heart.

Don't wait for someone else to validate what God has already promised you. Qualify yourself.

# In Your Creative Life

In your creative life, I give you permission to break the rules. You create your own reality, and there is nothing or anyone who can stop you from existing as a creative being.

**BE THE GREATEST.**

Keep dreaming & Stay focused on your purpose. Do that thing. Write that book. Start that business. Finish that degree. Design those clothes. Take that chance. This is your Life. #DoUBelieve #BETHEGREATEST

www.YdrateNelson.com

In your creative life, you don't have to look or dress a certain way unless you choose to. The uniqueness of your diverse wardrobe compliments the dynamics of your personality. You don't have to be any certain age or color.

In your creative life, you don't ever have to retire. There are no gender restrictions. You simply feel and express while using the arts that have been gifted to your spirit from the heavens.

## What are you really doing with this single life that God has gifted you with?

# Life Goes On

I have lost many people that are close to me, and those near and dear to my heart. I have been down and out, and deeply depressed. I have had thoughts of suicide and what it would be like if I was gone. While facing my own struggles, I had to learn that after every storm, there is sunshine.

It might be hard to see a blue sky while the storm rages, but the sunshine will appear regardless. I was down and out, but I am still here. I got hurt, but I am not afraid to love again. No matter what, tomorrow will come. This world doesn't stop. Life will always go on.

I can lie to the world, but I cannot lie to myself. I know that sometimes, I'll take a few losses before I win. Know that when you lose something—and you will—the way you recover is what defines you.

Life will always go on, and so remember that things take time, and everything is a process. Nothing happens overnight. Don't let grudges and anger block your blessings. Be forgiving and put things behind you. When you choose not to forgive and blame others for the pain you feel, you view the world with tainted vision and carry the baggage of the experience. Just let it go. No matter what happens today, yesterday, or tomorrow, know that life always goes on.

Don't fall victim to the expectations of other people. Design the life you desire to live based on what you expect of yourself. You are qualified.

# Make it Happen

For years, I talked about writing a book. I dreamed of having my works published and constantly wished I was an author. I did nothing. I just let my ideas pass as I wasted time and made excuses.

But not this time. I had to do something. I made a plan to share some of my creations with others in the spirit of inspiration. I processed that fact that life is limited, but the wisdom passed on is limitless.

I realized that the knowledge I have retained means nothing if I can't articulate the information to those who need it. I understand the value of leaving my daughter and family an eternal piece of life to hold on the day of my passing.

Frustrations and desperation forced me to act. I put actions behind my ambitions and made a plan to move forward with publishing a book. I adopted the theory of K.I.S. K.I.M—Keeping It Simple. Keeping It Moving. I didn't worry about what I could not do. I kept it simple and focused on all the things I knew could do. You are holding my plan in your hands in the form of a manifested dream that started as a simple thought.

This book started with one word, and it evolved all the way to a published work. Whether it's to write a book, start a business, live healthier, or travel the world, make a plan, make it plain, and make it happen.

# We Got Now

Too many of us are not enjoying our lives and aren't truly happy. It seems as if we are either caught up on something that has happened in the past or overly ambitious about the potential of what could happen in the future. Both scenarios are beyond control. The average person has about 2500 to 3500 thoughts per day, averaging about 14 seconds a thought. 90% of those thoughts are either focused on tomorrow or on yesterday.

However, instead of worrying about the past or the future, we must embrace the now—the opportunities that we have before us each and every second of our lives. We have to focus on what we have and not what we had or want. This mentality is about living *for* the present moment and living *in* the present moment.

Most of us are so ambitious that the desire to get ahead seems natural. We want to be famous, rich, powerful, or popular. We would rather have others envy us opposed to envying others. But ambition can make us focus on the goal ahead to the point where we forget to enjoy what we have in the moment. In the progressive world that we live in, we are always thinking about moving forward and planning for the future.

Most of us have a 401k plan, savings accounts, a dream home, or a dream car. And although goals, dreams, and aspirations are important, they often tear us away from our present. As a result, we are always thinking about more, but what about now? No, you don't have the job, the car, or the house you want, but you probably have a job of some sort, a car that gets you where you need to go, and shelter to keep you out of the elements.

You might not be the richest person, but I'll bet you live well. You might not be the most popular person, but I'll bet you have friends who delight and support you. If you focus on what's in front of you, everything else will come in time. Plan for tomorrow but live for today.

We have all been through some circumstance or situation that seemed unfair. It could have been a lost job, a bad relationship, the person who cut you off in traffic, or the person you work with you can't stand. Whatever the issue might be, we hold onto too many things that really don't matter. Regardless of whether it happened 5 years, 5 weeks, or 5 minutes ago, let it go. In fact, consider why you have a big windshield and small rearview mirrors. You can't drive forward looking back.

I remember when I would fly back home for the weekend and pack enough for an entire month. Most times, I wore the same clothes for the entire trip, frustrated that I lugged around all that baggage I didn't need.

When the airline started charging more for each bag, I learned to pack strategically and only take what I needed. That is what we must do in our lives. We must only travel with what we need and not carry around extra baggage. If we do, it comes with a great cost.

Too often, that cost is stress. According to information collected by the CDC in 2011, heart disease is the number one killer in America. The most common is coronary heart disease, which appears as a heart attack—induced by stress.

When we rush through life and carry burdens from the past, we create situations that end in frustrations, stress, and anger that often impact us negatively. When we become angry or stressed, our bodies experience a physical response to stress called a stressor.

And so, we start to produce adrenaline, we breathe faster, our heartbeats speed up, our blood pressure rises, muscle tension increases, our liver increase sugar output, and blood flow diverts to our brain and large muscles.

One minute of stress or anger creates an immune system deficiency for up to four to five hours where one minute of laughter stimulates us for 23 to 24 hours. So, let the stresses and anger go and be present today. Right now. It's time to focus on the fact that we have the present.

Don't use yesterday's greatness as an excuse not to be great today. Don't let the job you used to have or the salary you once made devalue the present opportunity you have. Whether you lost your home, your car got reposed, or your bills are past due, you must smile anyway because you have the present. The

BE THE GREATEST.

Embrace adversity head on and have faith that if you have survived every single thing that has come your way so far, there is nothing that can stop you. You are unstoppable. #DoUBelieve #BETHEGREATEST

www.YdrateNelson.com

past is gone. The future may never arrive. So don't ever forget that you have the *now.*

Words to Live By:

*Be yourself.*

*Love yourself.*

*Believe in yourself.*

# Soul Searching

For years, I thought there was a secret formula to becoming successful and rich. I believed other people had it but not me. However, I realized that there are important steps I needed to take to increase the likelihood of succeeding. To travel this path, I had to do some soul searching.

I started by praying and asking for God's help and guidance. I had to be completely honest with myself and had to make tough, life-changing decisions. During this process, I had to make choices between the wants of my personality and the needs of my soul.

Soul searching was a huge dose of reality for me. I had to face many things I didn't want to face. I felt embarrassment and shame for some of my past actions—and lack thereof. I discovered that I wasn't in control of my own life. I was responding to what life gave me as opposed to writing my own story. I was procrastinating and letting things happen to me, rather than making them happen.

I was stuck in my comfort zone and didn't take any calculated risks. The saddest part was that after this realization, I still didn't take immediate action to rectify the problem. It was as if the *check engine* light came on, but I refused to pop the hood and fix the problem. I just kept on driving. But one day, it all came down and I had no choice but to act.

# Live in the Moment

I fully embrace living in the moment with all the knowledge, history, and information from the past, and the infinite possibilities of the future. We must encourage each other in every way possible. We must maintain a positive mental attitude at all times. We must dig deep inside ourselves to discover who we are, where we are from, and where we are headed.

We can all free our souls and our minds, while using expressions and unique abilities that lie deep within our spirit. Whether it is artistic, physical, or psychological, we have all been blessed with a gift that can be used as an instrument of inspiration and self-fulfillment. It is up to us to find and pursue that unique ability, so we can free ourselves and define our purpose.

We must pass on the spirit of encouragement and kindness whenever we can. At some point, we will all need a helping hand and an encouraging word. Good karma is a lifestyle. We must motivate each other on spiritual levels in hopes of elevating our personal levels of achievement.

We must increase self-love, self-confidence, and promote unity to improve our quality of life. We have obligations to ourselves to make the world a little better. We must stick together, particularly when times get hard. Strength stands in numbers, and love conquers all. We must plan our work, then execute it with precision.

Now is the time to make a plan and act. All we have are the moments that we live in. Let's make those seconds count in the best ways we can. We have the *now.*

# Anything is Possible if you Believe

**BE THE GREATEST.**

Go get it. Set a goal, map it out and make it happen. It's time to make plays not excuses. #DoUBelieve #BETHEGREATEST

www.YdrateNelson.com

I was walking through life wishing for my dreams to come true. I was looking for riches and success as if I'd lost them somewhere. But I was looking for something that was never mine and I couldn't find it because I was living based on the standards of other people.

I bought someone else's dream and failed to realize my own. I was trying to be like the things I saw in the media, in my friends, and on TV. I had no passion about my state of being and I had no direction, either. This left me spinning my wheels and wasting my life away.

And so, I decided to pursue my own destiny and take control of my life. I wanted to travel down the path of happiness and prosperity. I was fed up with feelings of anger and frustration. I was tired of doing what everybody else was doing. It was time for a change.

# Learning to trust myself

It took time before I started developing a personal level of growth where I was able to listen and trust myself. I had to learn to put all my trust in God and let His spirit and love consume me until my being was recreated in the likeness of the Most High.

At first, I had no self-discipline or true relationship with God. But with time, I finally identified the purposes the creator had for me and found reason behind my actions, which fueled a passion in me that made me want to live life to the fullest. Every day, I remind myself, "You can have anything you want."

I now know that my success and happiness have nothing to do with money or what I have in my possession. Success comes when I achieve the goals that I set for myself and happiness comes from my mindset and outlook on the present, past, and future. Note to self: Success happens day by day, one step at a time—not always when and where you think it should be.

# Another Chapter

Each day you live creates another chapter in your book of life. Even though past chapters exist, they don't dictate the chapters that lie before you. No matter what you've done or who you are, there is always something more waiting to be written. You could retire, but the book wouldn't be over.

You could be the leader of the whole free world, but there will always be something more that needs to be done. You could be the richest person on earth but still have more to conquer. Age is not a factor. You are never too old to do anything you set your mind to.

Colonel Sanders from Kentucky took his social security check at the age of 65 and set out to turn Kentucky Fried Chicken into a franchise. His story was not over. He simply moved on to a new chapter. This applies to each of us. Go back to school or start that new business today and write your next chapter. Don't wait.

There's nothing that can stop you from redeeming yourself at any point in your life. You could be homeless, jobless, heartbroken, or forgotten about, but there will still another chapter waiting to be written. We've all experienced extreme lows in your lives that made it seem our book was closed, and that the ink had dried. But this isn't the case. My grandmother used to say, "I have never seen a storm last forever." She never said there were no storms.

We have to remember not to end our own story and close our own book. We can't afford to allow one chapter to tell our entire story. We are the authors of our every moment, and we can decide how our books turn out. We can change a story that people thought they knew the ending to, simply by deciding to. I urge you not to let anybody or anything take that away from you.

# Let the Past be the Past

I wasted many days of my life holding myself back because I was holding onto things that I couldn't change. I was allowing the pain from the past to stop me from moving on. If I injured my knee, I started fearing running altogether. I missed so my opportunities because of issues and circumstances that I let control me. I was holding onto heartaches, the deaths of loved ones, broken promises, and so much more.

These simple things made my life a living hell because they kept me re-living the negative experiences that were over and forced me into a mindset of self-pity. I was the further from optimistic and allowed my positive thoughts to be dominated by the dark thoughts of my past. I knew I had to find a way to free my mind and let the past be the past.

It often seems impossible to move on from events that occurred in our past. We sometimes feel we can never forget the things that have happened to us. And although we may never forget, we surely can move on.

I remember the first time I had my heart broken. I was in love with a woman who was everything I ever could ask for. She was smart, witty, and beautiful—inside and out. I was convinced that she was my soulmate. Then, one day, she broke up with me. I cried countless nights over her. For years, I lived in hurt and pain.

I felt sorry for myself and found an endless number of reasons to blame myself for the breakup. But I was missing out on all the wonderful things that were right before my eyes. I allowed my past to dictate my present and my future. I allowed the old to block the new.

One day, I came to a realization that I was not the only person living with pain and hurt. There were many others who had suffered a great lost and they got passed it. I could, too. I was trying to forget about the loss and suffering and started to heal slowly.

I learned to appreciate the negative things I was feeling and used them to develop empathy and understanding. Had I not had my heart crushed into a million pieces, I never would have developed a major part of my personality that contributed to who I am today. We may never be able to forget the pain of the past but can instead use it to become better.

We have all experienced bad business deals, lies, deaths, heartaches, and break ups. But it is time to let it go. Someone stole from you? Let it go. You were lied to? Let it go. Somebody betrayed you? Let it go.

The hardest of all is the loss of a loved one, but you have to let it go so you can move closer to what is in store for you. I have held onto death for so long to the point where I was dragging myself closer to the grave with my own negative thoughts and actions. I had to learn to move on because sitting in misery is not what we are intended to do. The scripture says, "Weeping may endure for the night, but joy is coming in the morning." You may feel pain, but you will rejoice again. We all will.

Sometimes, to move on from the past, you will have to revisit the past first. Some things need to be dealt with head-on before they can be dismissed. When I look at the life I have lived and all the things I have done, it seems impossible to clean it all up. But I know that some things need to be addressed and some things just need to be let go.

There are so many small things that we can hold onto, but the reality is we shouldn't. Let it go. Free yourself from the past and run toward your destiny.

The past is just that: the past. I will continue to learn from all experiences whether perceived to be good or bad because I know the darkest nights are needed to understand and appreciate the brightest days. I will stop wasting time. I will stop complaining about it, talking about it, and wishing for it. It's time to get it done. No more excuses.

# No More Excuses

## *No More Excuses*

I am not going to let where I am

from, the color of my skin, or my

level education be an excuse for

not doing whatever my mind can

perceive. Excuses are gateways

to procrastination, which is the

enemy of productivity. The time

spent complaining could be used

to make a plan of action.

# Count Your Blessings

It's a blessing to see another day. It's a blessing for me to write these words and for you to read them. Some many blessings pass us each day without a conscious thought. When we don't realize the blessings we have, we are less likely to bless others. At this point, we aren't getting the most out of life or living up to our full potential because we are putting out our best. We rob ourselves of our true happiness and fulfillment. All it takes is a shift in our conscious mind frame and awareness to overcome this.

When we realize the many blessings we have, we can find our purpose. If we understand and process the fact that we woke up this morning and many people didn't, that in itself is a blessing. If we can walk and get ready for work, that in itself is a blessing. If we have a reliable car to get us where we need to go, that in itself is a blessing.

These blessings are in front of us. Many times, we don't pause to say thank you and appreciate what we have before we focus on what we don't. When we focus on the blessings, our joys will be magnified. When we're aware of our blessings, we can see God's abundance, which induces a spirit of giving. This giving and passing of blessing starts a new cycle that motivates and inspires others to do the same. In the challenging economic times of the world, we live in, many people are turned off by giving because of the perception that giving has to be financial. We give little when we give of our possessions, but the giving of our time is priceless.

# Time Is Ticking Away

We have 168 hours per week. That is 10,800 minutes and 604,800 seconds. That is our constant. We can't change that. We can change the variables—what we do with the time—but we cannot change the time itself.

There is time for us to do anything we choose. Every second of time is precious—use it wisely. Forget wasted time in the past and do something new today. Do it now. Make a new plan, write it down, and make it happen. It's your time. Take control.

You determine what and how you feel. Don't let what another person thinks of you stop you from doing what you have to do. Your time is ticking. All of our time is ticking. Whatever you have in mind, do it. Do it now.

# Live In Faith Everyday
# (LIFE)

Being who I am, doing what I want, and making a living to support my family is my idea of ultimate success. Like everything in life, this is a process, takes time, and grows day by day. My first step was making the choice to pursue my own destiny. We all have our own path to travel and what is best for one man might not be best for the next. It is up to us as individuals to find what is meant for us. Believe what you feel is worth believing in, and keep in mind that knowing is one thing but acting on it is another.

Things would be a lot harder for us if we did not have other people to assist us on our journey. Nobody goes through life alone. We much learn to help one another and work together. We must encourage each other and speak positively about each other. We must help others win and take pride in their victories. We must not think negatively about each other, particularly before we get the chance to know the person in front of us.

We must find search for ways to bring our ideas to life, rather than settle on ways that will make our ideas fail. We must share the things we value most with others. We must give from the heart knowing that it will come back to us in the form of blessings. We must surround ourselves with others who understand how we feel and can share our dreams and aspirations. Establish a team of associates with wisdom, knowledge, and integrity you respect.

Together, as a team, stand strong and operate in faith. No matter how bad things may get, never give up on one another.

An effective way that I've found to stay inspired is to surround yourself with those who are successful. Stay away from ignorant, negative, and jealous people who try to rain on your parade because they don't have one of their own. Seek the positive and inspirational souls who are successful in some way.

Learn from these people and their experiences and take the time to plan and execute. Write down your goals and make them visible. Develop them from a thought to plan to a reality. Writing things down allows us to focus more the goal instead of treating it as a passing thought.

Once goals are visible, they become external, and you can see the solutions from a universal perspective. Don't be afraid to change the plan or make adjustments as you go. Everything changes. Things happen and you never know what tomorrow will bring. Keep your updated goals posted so you can see the progress and remain focused. Too many foolish things distract your brain in a day, and you need to be constantly reminded of your goals. It will keep you focused.

You never know when something major will happen in your life, and so, you have to be prepared every day. You have to use the knowledge you acquire. It does not take a college degree to execute an effective plan. Make sure you have the right balance to maintain your goal physically, mentally, and spiritually. You need time to work on each individual aspect of your life. Invest time, don't just spend time. Time is valuable and time management is essential. By investing time, you will become a valuable resource.

We have to train our minds to be on the lookout for situations that could lead to opportunity. This will allow you to see opportunity when you would not normally see it and even help create it when it is needed. We must take actions demanding success and achievement. When things don't go as planned, we cannot blame others.

We have to take responsibility for our actions, which will lead us to gain more confidence to take risks. The main thing people fear is the unknown and this leads to not taking risks. You have to take a chance to pursue what you believe in, or you will never truly be fulfilled.

I had to learn to trust myself. I felt like I had to master keeping promises to myself so keeping promises to others would be a simpler task. When you help your own secrets to yourself, you have no obligation to another soul and no one to punish you if you don't follow through.

The first step to making a promise is trusting that you will follow through on it. If you don't trust yourself, it will be impossible to trust anyone else. And so, building self-trust is the foundation of commitment. Stick to your goals until you see them through and enforce repercussions for not following through. Only when you learn to be committed to yourself first can you appreciate what it means to keep your word to others.

In life, we will never truly be a success until we are happy with who we are. The day starts and ends with you in every situation. No one can manifest your dreams but you. Don't wait for anyone to give you an encouraging word because you may never

get it. Encourage yourself and others and you will get it back. Don'
ever give up. Always keep your faith. It is never too late to start
anything. The sooner you get started, the sooner you arrive. On our
quest to reach ultimate success, there are no secrets that
guarantee prosperity, but there are things we can do to increase
the likelihood of succeeding. If you aren't happy with yourself, you
will never truly be happy.

# All for the Love

There is nothing more rewarding than doing what you love to do and not having to worry about money. Many forms of art have been lost in the shuffle for the sake of the dollar. I give me to the wolrd in the purest form for the love of what I do.

In a capitalistic system, more money equals more power. But money only represents external power. Internal power comes from within when you are the person the Most-High intended you to be. I don't do what I do for the sake of the dollar.

I do what I love knowing I will be compensated in more ways than money can provide. I understand and recognize that money is not worth  compromising my personal freedom or integrity for.

Everything costs something, and most of the the time, it is time, it's time itself that's spent. There is nothing more valuable than time. So, when you think about a purchase, an investment, or a destination, think about the time you would spend on it. Money can be gained or lost, but the time it takes to generate money is only worth investing if you can get more than just a dollar in return.

If you are not doing what you love, you can never be happy. I have found my happiness in forms that no dollar could ever buy or take from me.

# Before you look at me

We encounter many people in our lifetime. We learn many names and recognize many faces. But we never see our own. We only see reflections of our face when we look in mirrors. We can see our pictures, images, and videos, but nothing more.

And so, we have to trust the reflection. But what if the mirror that we look through lies? What if what the mirror shows us is not the same thing that the rest of the world sees? We could be living a lie and not even know it.

We look at images that are tainted by the perception of the world. The universe does not see us the way we see ourselves. The third eye is the only eye that really counts. If it is closed open it. If it is lost find it. If it is tainted, purify it.

But before you look at anyone else, you really need to look at yourself. We're often too quick to judge others, but we can't point a finger at someone else without pointed 3 more back at ourselves.

# We Are All Seeds

My grandfather was a farmer. As a young child, the majority of food we had come from my grandfather's garden. Each year, he starts out with all the seeds, and before we knew, we had food to put on the table. Most of the time, I never considered the process that each seed had to go through to produce fruit. Once we consider this process, we can also consider and recognize that we are all seeds, growing every day. In case you fail to realize the process, let me share my experience as a seed.

Can you imagine being buried in darkness deep below the earth? No one has any idea you even exist. Before the first sprout breaks the surface, the growing process is underway. Before breaking the dirt, a seed must grow down deeper into the cold and darkness. The deeper the seed grows, the stronger its roots will be, which provide all support and store the food that will soon bloom. Strong roots are a vital aspect to survival. The type and depth of the roots grow depending on the kind of seeds planted. A corn stalk, for example, would never have roots as strong as those of an oak tree.

No matter what seed is planted, all require rain and sunshine for growth. Sometimes, you get just enough rain and just enough sunshine, but sometimes, you get too much of either. As a result, many seeds get washed away or dried out completely. That is why strong roots are vital. If a seed is given too much heat, it will be able to use stored materials to continue growing. If there is a surplus of running water, the roots will serve as an anchor to keep the seed from getting caught in the wash.

After sitting in darkness, a seed's process is unrecognized by the world, until the surface is broken and light shines. When a sprout finally breaks the surface, a new set of challenges comes afterward. The plant has to fight the harsh conditions of nature and the weeds that try to choke it out. Then, there are natural causes, animals, and insects that make the growth process even harder. Still, roots keep the plant alive. As it continues to reach higher for the sky, the roots must continue to grow down to be able to support the extra weight from the developing seed.

In the mature stages of growth, a seed begins to develop stems. These stems develop into branches, each with more and more stems growing. The branches are connected to the trunk, and the trunk runs back to the roots that hold down the structure. Then, fruit emerges. Within the fruit, there is sweetness—the rewards of the growth process. Within the fruit are more seeds that will start the process over again.

We are all seeds, and we all have our own growth process. Even when we bear fruit, we will never stop growing. And when we get the chance to taste the sweetness of the fruit, we must ensure to never forget about the process that it took to grow. Don't ever forget the seeds that started the growth process and remember the roots that anchor us and keeps us grounded. We are all seeds.

# Free Yourself

## *Free Yourself*

Many times, I allowed past events to burden me. I allowed my regrets to weigh me down. I allowed my past to dictate my present and alter my future.

All I could think about were the things I wished I could change, but simply couldn't. I compromised my own joy, draining myself of all my emotional strength. The sad part was I didn't even know it.

Then, one day, I had a realization. I had to commit to myself. I made an inner and personal declaration to free myself from the shackles that are keeping me grounded.

# My Declaration of Independence

I am neither afraid of the future nor ashamed of the past. I accept the reality of my imperfections. I cannot change anything but my present state. I have turned my regrets into learning experiences. I am taking charge of my destiny. I am taking control of my life by focusing my energies toward completing tasks guilt-free.

I am learning to achieve by progressively growing and problem-solving new ways to reach my goals. No matter what obstacles I face, I will count it all joy. This is the foundation of my vision. I am putting the past behind me and moving forward in physical and mental progression.

Follow my steps and free yourself.

# III...Poetic Expressions

Poetry saved my life.

# Poetry to me

A poem can be a long, complex series of verses connected with verbs and nouns, metaphorically combined to capture the essence of an emotion. A poem can be as simple as one word that sums up a thought. Some poems might rhyme, and some might not. Some have deeper meanings and require time spent in a pensive state, while others are straight-forward.

Some may require you to read the words over and over, finding new meaning each time. Some may only need to be read or hear once. Sometimes poetry can inspire you to laugh and sometimes it can cause you to cry. Poetry can make you feel love and it can make you feel hate. But most of all, a good poem will simply make you feel.

We are all poets, and we write many poems each day. We may not write them down, but we create the material through life's experiences—the blueprint for future generations to build on. We must keep a record of what we do to monitor our growth and create our legacy. I chose to use poetry as a platform to speak what I feel.

The essence of poetry to me is to seek it, understand it, create it, and inspire another to do the same. Poetry is more than words on paper. It sets my mind free and allows me to express the things I truly feel and think. I use my poetic ability to capture the realities of life and the feelings and thoughts I experience every step of the way. Without poetry, my life would be a blur of cluttered thoughts.

I have no intention to be recognized as the greatest poet of all time, rather I want to let the world see my inner realm of hurt, pain, love, and growth—all of which have groomed me into the man I am today. Some of my work might resonate with you, while some of it might not. I encourage you keep an open mind, respect my art, and respect my life as a poet and a person.

There are no criteria to who can and cannot be a poet, or what can and cannot be considered poetic. The only criteria is that you *feel*. The words and expressions you use to convey how you feel is poetry in and of itself. Just capture the essence of the emotion, whether you choose to do so through written or spoken word, it will be powerful. Be conscious of what you say but never compromise what you feel. Poetry can surely be a form of entertainment, but to me, it's an outlet.

From the good times to the heartbreaks, I try to capture as many emotions as possible. My job is not to make you understand everything I say, but rather to accurately represent what and how I feel. Each work of art is a seed that I planted and helped grow. These are my inner thoughts and emotions. This is me.

# Everybody and Nobody

Everybody wants to be the boss,
Nobody wants the responsibility.

Everybody wants the glory of a good deed,
Nobody wants the responsibility of the failure.

Everybody wants to be rich and famous,
Nobody wants to work for the fame or riches.

Everybody wants the accolades of the hero,
Nobody wants the realistic label of the villain.

Everybody wants to be at the top,
Nobody wants to take the first step.

Everybody wants to be known for greatness,
Nobody wants to be forgotten or overlooked.

Everybody wants to be loved and adored,
Nobody wants to be hated or criticized.

Everybody wants to get paid,
Nobody wants to pay dues.

Everybody wants to be self-sufficient,
Nobody makes it alone.

Everybody knows good things come to those who wait,
But nobody wants to wait.

I am everybody
and I am nobody.

# Be Strong

A sense of hopelessness and desperation
seems to be the root of my life's frustrations.
Trying hard to avoid jeopardizing situations,
on my quest to manifest
reality out of these dreams I am chasing.

Negativity for positivity is worth replacing,
being patient in the dark
as I wait for my chance to shine,
even when I feel stagnant as if I've fallen behind.

Yet, I still continue to work and wait,
avoiding negative thinking and shifting my state of mind.
My life and my fate are all in His hands,
continuously moving across these burning sands.

Many things in this life I will never understand,
and I understand that as just part of being a man,
as I continue my mission, eyes focused on the vision,
not about life's options, but on my own decisions.

From birth to death, we take many first steps.
We love independence, but we all need help.
As I continue to search for those missing links,
focus on the goal, no matter what others think.

Even when I am down, I will never be out.
One road doesn't work, I create another route.

Holding on no matter what's going on,
mentally, physical, and spiritually
is where I must remain strong.

*Inspiration*: *I wrote this in Hawaii, in June of 2000 while visiting my father. I was reflecting on the frustrations behind me, and the chance before me to prosper. I walked out on the patio, looking at the beautiful scene, and started to write. And so, this was born.*

# At Worst if I Fall

This world is no friend to me,

my mind is gone. I have suicidal tendencies.


I can't take all this pain I feel in my soul,

seems like it's easier to let it all go.


Man, I'm out, because it's got to be a better place.

I think I'm losing. Why the hell am I in this race?


I think I'm lost, trying my best to find a way home,

getting weak, trying my best just to stay strong.


I can't sleep when the devil is plaguing my dreams,

tossing and turning, but nobody can hear my scream.


I think he's got me, trying my best just to get loose.

It's a struggle, but man, I refuse.


To give up, I came way too far.

I had dreams one day I would be a star.

I don't shine, my mind is in relapse,

mind, body, and soul are all trapped.

I want to go where these worries don't exist,

I wish my momma would have told me about days like this.

But she didn't, and I am learning the hard way,

getting weak, trying to find where the Lord stays.

Is He home, or did I knock at the right house?

I'm at the fork, wondering, did I take the right route?

I don't know. Down and out these evils kept me,

got me begging, please somebody help me...

I wrote this poem when I was depressed and sad. I was at a very low point. One of my closest friends had been killed, and I remember waking up and realizing I was crying in my sleep. I woke up, grabbed a pen, and wrote this.

# Still Here

I have been shot at by those who wanted to kill me.

I have been lied to by those who don't know me.

I have been deceived by those I trusted.

I have been misunderstood by those who don't get me.

I have been discriminated against by those who   prejudged me.

But by the grace of God, none of that took me out.

I am still who I am, and I am still here.

# I Prayed

I prayed for love, and hatred found me.

I prayed for peace, and a war broke out.

I prayed for support, and found myself alone.

I prayed for patience, and I was pushed to my limit.

I prayed for strength, and found my weaknesses.

I prayed for answers, and found new questions.

I prayed for guidance, and found myself lost.

I prayed for mercy, and found merciless situations before me.

I Prayed for prosperity, and found myself amid a deficit.

I prayed for others, and now I am in need of prayer.

I prayed for many situations, and God challenged me with the opportunity to grow.

*What are you praying for?*

# God Spoke to Me

God spoke to me
But I didn't want to hear what He had to say.
Instead of listening, I turned and walked away.

I tried to pretend like I didn't even hear,
knowing good and well, I heard it loud and clear.

Conflicted inside, most can't even see my struggle.
Outside, it's a smile, deep down, I am in trouble.

God is calling me to work for His kingdom,
but I neglected the work so I could have earthly fun.

I love the life with little responsibility,
but the truth is, my actions are killing me.

Sinking ship every single day,
my heart is telling me that God is the way.

Personality calling me to do the things that I like,
while God's perfect grace protects me, despite
all my flaws. Wait, I'm coming, I'm just not quite ready yet.
Every second is another one that can't be replaced,
guilty of mismanagement—what a waste.

Waiting for my mind to catch my spirit,
I am hurting, crying out, but nobody can hear it.
All I have in this world is my word and my faith,
as I struggle to make that transition, hope I'm not too late.

# Just...Be

Be Still. Be Creative. Be Free. Be Positive. Be Courageous. Be Grateful. Be Peaceful. Be Love. Be Kind. Be Responsible for your vision. Be Amazing. Be You.

We are always looking to do way more than *just be*. You are not what you do. We are not human havings, human doings, or human makings. We are human beings. You are what you *be*. Sometimes, you have to *just be*.

---

*Don't ever let another person tell you what you can or cannot do, or what you can or cannot be. Do and be you.*

# Have You Ever

*Have you ever*
Been so happy, you wanted to cry?
Felt so alive when you thought you were going to die?
Been so mad, you had to laugh?
Deserved it all, and didn't get half?

*Have you ever*
Looked in the mirror, and didn't see yourself?
Had your priorities right, but steered to the left?
Been so upset, you couldn't even breathe?
Had to go, but didn't want to leave?

*Have you ever*
Been so broke, you saw no fix?
Unwrapped the tootsie roll and wondered how many licks?
Looked at the stars, and wondered how far away?
Had a mind full of thoughts, but didn't know what to say?

*Have you ever*
Wanted to go, but had to stay?
Struggled through the night to see another day?
Had the chance, but let it slip away?
Should have been free, but you had to pay?

*Have you ever*
Been so hot, you forgot the cool?
Knew the answer, but felt like a fool?
Been so cold, you forgot the heat?
Been so bitter, you forgot the sweet?

*Have you ever*

Been so far, you could see no close?

Did the least, but got the most?

Been so trapped, you forgot the free?

Took care of everybody, just to forget the me?

*Inspired by: Tears of joy. When they saw my tears and asked me what was wrong, I replied. "Have you Ever... Been so happy that you cried..."*

# What's Life?

Is life just a pitstop

while traveling through eternity,

or is it like the end of a night,

like blowing out the light?

When the pain stops

and the good memories roll,

the works I have done speak for me,

 and others bless my soul.

And when the deeds speak,

what will they say?

Did I prepare for the journey

or live for the day?

Was the picture pretty,

or images of the flaw

memories from people

who claim they say?

The actions that prevailed

as my life unfolds,

from the options you had

and the things I chose.

How much time spent
on chasing the wealth,
how much time spent
on preservation of the self?

No more walking the lines
between love and hate,
the next decisions made
are at the judgment gate.

The concept of time
no longer exists,
time to enter the land
of the righteousness.

When the time comes,
will I be prepared?
Will all fears be lifted,
with no reason to be scared?

Wondering, is there a soul inside
or just flesh and blood?
Will it really matter between
the bad and the good?

Who would miss me

or be glad I am gone?

Who is the next king

to take over the throne?

The goals I set,

did I achieve?

Did I inspire the world

and make others believe?

Was the ride too short,

or just long enough?

Did my spirit keep striving,

and I didn't give up?

Was this day bound,

or happen out of the blues?

Was it one big dream,

or was it really all true?

Will God answer the door

when I knock?

Will my soul live on,

as the flesh continues to rot?

# I Am Sorry.

Sorry for all the lies I told
Sorry for everything I ever stole

Sorry for all the pain I caused
Sorry to all the friends I have lost.

Sorry for all my greed
Sorry to my aborted seeds

Sorry for not being a better friend
Sorry for every time I sinned.

Sorry for not being a better brother
Sorry for not being a better lover

Sorry for not being a better son
Sorry for all the bad I have done.

Sorry for the time I forgot about God
Sorry for quitting when things got hard

Sorry for not expressing my love
I have taken it up with the man above.

I am sorry.

# Forever Lives My Soul

Don't cry for me,
I have lived my life.
God has truly blessed me,
I taught my children to walk upright.

It was just my time,
Father called me home.
I am forever with you,
you shall never be alone.

The lessons you have learned,
will be with you all your days.
The spirit of me is in you,
and so, you shall always find your way.

There will be days ahead,
when the tears will flow.
It's okay to feel the sorrow,
it's okay to let it go.

When the sadness visits,
don't let it consume you.
Just know I am with you,
in all that you do.

I will be with you, watching
with a bird's eye view from above.
Protecting God's children,
with the spirit of eternal love.

Stand tall and proud,
lifting your head high.
In the spirit of my life,
tie a ribbon in the sky.

Remember to reflect
on all the good days,
holding those memories close.
It's just my physical body that is resting,
and forever lives my soul.

# The Acknowledgement

*The Inspiration: My first heartbreak poem.* I was so sad and felt
like there was no one to talk to. I picked up a piece of paper and
this what I wrote. It was one of the most liberating things I ever
wrote.

Dancing in innocent hearts
leaves aches in the center of the soul.
Karma returns the favor,
bringing division amongst the once whole.
Time is of the essence,

when jousting with her hands.
If situations can't be moved,
settle them where they stand.
Without a plan,

free spirits move lost in the universe.
Distrust and confusion make love a curse,
even worse,

if you don't stick
open wounds gap and bleed.
The first step to healing
 is acknowledging the need.

# My Heart, My Mind

*The Inspiration: I met one of the most physically beautiful women I have ever encountered. I couldn't even believe she was into me. She was good for my ego, but bad for my spirit. I am now dealing with the wants of my personality, versus the needs of my soul.*

My mind says: this chick is crazy.

My heart says: wow, she's amazing.

My mind says: free yourself, let her go.

My heart says: free yourself, hold her, and hold her close.

My mind says: this is way too much.

My heart says: I just can't get enough.

My mind says: I don't need this stress.

My heart says: without her, my spirit doesn't rest.

My mind says: why do I deal with this?

My heart says: please set me free with a gentle kiss.

My mind says: I don't want to fight.

My heart says: if loving you is wrong, I don't want to be right.

My mind says: the confusion is not worth it.

My heart says: no relationship is perfect.

My mind says: there are plenty of fish in the sea.

My heart says: she is the only one for me.

But I still had to let her be.

# A Better Day

All my dreams are gone,

All my decisions seem wrong.

I still hold on and remain strong,

But these days are long.

New days, same old song,

Still not being heard.

As my mind elevates

like migrating birds,

Seeking the word

to help me see a better day.


*Written in 2001. There have been times when I hated my life and lost sight of who I really was. Things seemed so complex and crazy that I wished I could just be alone, away from the problems, people, and confusion. Sometimes, it seemed as if death was a better option than life. No more worries, no more suffering, no more pain, just peace and tranquility.*

*Thank God for Deliverance.*

# A Silent Cry

I want it,

I need it,

I live for it,

I will die without it,

comforts me when I'm alone,

satisfies my craving desires,

makes me happy when I am sad,

I don't know how I ever made it before,

the best friend I ever had,

I am addicted,

Help.


*Written in 2006.*

# Strength and Unity

Thanking the lord for the sun and the rain,
learning from the past
to see what tomorrow might bring.

As I listen to the words from the flesh and blood,
when the rain hits the dirt
we get nothing but mud.

Before the water can cleanse,
the dirt must be swept.
Knowledge must be absorbed,
but must not be kept.

From those of who do not know,
it will be the fault of the educated
if we don't show.

The light to those who are kept in the dark,
forest fires start from one spark.

Tall trees grow from one seed,
the ability to educate
has already met the need.

Being educated has to become priority,
flesh taking the righteous path
seems to be the minority.

Traveling a path
that gets the majority lost,
we don't need coins

to pay the cost.

Glorify the works
that lead to higher understanding,
but sacrifice is needed
to achieve these things,
that have been gifted to us
by the creator.
Now is the time,
we may never see later.

Before the world takes over,
we must reach the youth.
Make them aware of the lies,
and finally tell the truth.

The bigger picture draws hope
for a better tomorrow,
trials and tribulation will occur,
there's no need for sorrow.

Before tasting the sweet nectar
of the fruits,
observe the tree
and the origin of its roots.
For preservation
and to rebuild our community,
stand strong in belief
and always live in unity.

*Written in 2005. We can all make it. Just not by ourselves.*

# Before You Leap

You have to look before you leap,
but sometimes jump on faith.
Don't get fooled by aromas
that smell good with a bitter taste.

To move life's mountains,
take it a stone at a time.
Some things are better off aged
like cognac and fine wine.

Sometimes it's okay
to color outside the line,
home is not a place,
it's a state of mind.

Accept life's setbacks
with style and grace,
even the quiet times
have their place.
Life is too short
to hold grudges and anger,
let them pass by like
negativity, short days, and strangers.

Never ever settle for second best,
it makes no sense,
like studying for a drug test.

When my plate gets full,
I share my leftovers.

Can't be in a drunk state of mind,
when you are sober.

Keep moving the goal post
and achieve more than ever thought,
with victories in battles
before the wars are even fought.

Keep living and loving,
exploring hidden talents,
longevity holds the key to success,
so, accept the challenge.

The bigger picture can't be seen on TV,
opportunities in faces like pimples in 3D.

When the weather gets cloudy,
make sure it's a short storm,
with bells of ideas ringing
like church bells and freedom.

I tried the seed, money don't grow on trees,
just a misunderstood flower,
not your ordinary weed.

Wear so many hats my head stays covered,
I was born in the dirt, so I can rise above it.

Nothing is perfect, so
no need to be reminded.
Not afraid of the search,
just deal with the finding.

Some unpopular decisions

have to be made for our own good.
It's time to make moves,
instead of wishing that I could.

*Written in June 2000. Inspired by the thought of taking a leap of faith, doing something grand, and not living with regrets.*

# Words From My Father

Be Humble

Be Respectful

Be Empathetic

Be Cool

Allow Laughter

Hand drawn by my father Donald Thomas Sr. in the early 80's. Now I see my daughter Eden with artistic ambitions, and it makes perfect sense.

# The Some of Things

Some people do, some people don't.
Some people will, some people won't.

Some gon' love, some gon' hate.
Some do it now, and some gon' wait.

Some gon' help, some gon' oppose.
Some are ladies, and some are hoes.

Some gon' think before they react,
Some gon' think after the fact.

Some gon' do it, some gon' talk.
Some gon' ride, and some gon' walk.

Some gon' like, some gon' diss.
Some understand, and some get pissed.

Some gon' exist, and some gon' live.
Some are selfish, and some give a rib.

Some gon' touch, and some gon' feel.
Some gon' play, and some just deal.

Some gon' look, and some gon' observe.
Some are straight and narrow, while some gon' swerve.

Some gon' read, and some gon' absorb.

Some hold back, and some go forward.

Some gon' listen, and some gon' hear.
Some are bold, and some gon' fear.

Some gon' miss, and some gon' understand.
Some wait for it, and some make a plan.

Some gon' reflect, and some gon' think.
Some gon' eat, and some gon' drink.

Some gon' talk, and some say something.
Some got it all, and some got nothing.

Some give the answer, and some ask the questions.
Some say nothing, while some make all the suggestions.

Some speculate, and some believe.
Some gon' wish, and some gon' achieve.

*Written in 2002. Add up the some of things and see if you can calculate where you fit.*

# The Will

Life is a funny thing, and time brings change.
You just never know what tomorrow holds.
Will I lose another friend or find my wife?
Will my future become secured, or will I lose my life?

Will the sun shine or is there a forecast of rain?
Will all my sins be washed away without a stain?
Will someone I love enter the next world?
Will a young lady evolve from an old girl?

Will the wars of the world finally be over?
Will the alcoholics commit to being sober?
Will someone catch me if I fall?
Will the job I applied for give me a call?

Will Jesus come back for those who believe?
Will the illiterate make the decision to read?
Will the government provide shelter for the homeless?
Will the bigots of the world no longer be bias?

Will a pregnant mother abort her unborn seed?
Will more of our youth die because of greed?
Will the dues of the game finally be paid?
Will someone having unprotected sex get aids?

Will there be another attack in the land of the brave?
Will the government decide we should again be slaves?
Will the thunder role and the lightning strike?
Will more decide to do wrong instead of right?

Will more sinners decide to become preachers?
Will the students stand up and become the teachers?
Will the virgins of the world decide to give it up?
Will conservative souls decide it's time to live it up?
Will I lose a limb or find myself?

140

Will I trade my poor righteous honor
for greed and filthy wealth?

*Written in 2002, inspired by the Some of Things.*

# Destined for Greatness

We are destined for greatness.

We can accept what we have

but never settle for who or what we are.

We can always grow

We can always get better

Why settle for good

when better is possible?

We are destined for greatness!

# My Black Man Vent

The spirit of the confederacy ain't dead,

but they're not marching with hoods on their head.

They have uniforms, robes, badges, and suites instead,

smiling in your face before they pull that trigger,

with hate in their heart, screaming, "My nigga!"

Then we march in peace and nonviolence,

but they don't hear us until we riot.

Now we're a threat, crazy, and lazy,

when all we're doing is trying to protect our babies.

We were born here and taught to love this nation,

but there is no replication with this mass incarceration,

of those with roots that trace back to African nations,

more Blacks in prison today than in slavery in 1850.

Before the judge sees me, society says that I am guilty.

The system is filthy,

I am a reflection of how America built me.

They say America is the only nation that is free,

but I am not sure that applies to guys that look like me.

Or my son,

You need evidence: Eric Gardner, Mike Brown, and Trayvon.

How China got more than a billion people than us,

but we got more people locked up, something seems wrong.

More Blacks in American jails than in the entire prison system
in Russia.

They kill us to hush us.

Now we're supposed to trust these cops,

when I have stood in the spot where BIG and Pac got shot.

It doesn't seem like a priority to figure out

what happened to these brothers, and they're famous.

What about people like me who are nameless?

The big picture is frameless.

Now I hide my pride to avoid being crucified

by another justified homicide.

I can't afford to be covered in that white sheet,

or have my spirits killed as I sit in that back seat.

Based on what another Black man did,

the label is placed on me.

But only if it is negative attention,

the positive things do not even get mentioned.

But that makes no sense,

only associate my skin and kin with *thug*,

when there is a Black man president,

but I guess that's irrelevant.

Oh, to hell with it.

I just needed to vent.

# Giving Thanks

It's a must that I give thanks to the Almighty and the Most-High, God. I believe in glory over defeat. I am so blessed and truly grateful. This is just a book with my words. The bible is the book, and God has the ultimate word.

I thank you so much for taking a moment out of your life so I could share a piece of mine with you. I realize you could be doing several other things, but are right here, right now. I am grateful.

I am sharing a lot more than words and thoughts. This is my vision being manifested right before your eyes. With deepest gratitude, thank you so much for your time and support. I now know in my heart that, if I die today, I will live forever. Thank You and thank God.

*What are you thankful for?*

# FROM ME TO YOU.

*Thank you. I appreciate you. I love you. God Bless you. Now it is time for you to write your book. Let's get started.*

The mission of **BE THE GREATEST (BTG)** is leverage education, fashion, influence and entertainment to inspire higher achievement, increase self esteem and maximize personal Greatness.

BETHEGREATEST.co

YdrateNelson.com

The mission of YNA is to be a global leader in the motivation, coaching and education industries, building relationships on a passion for serving, living a motivated lifestyle and striving for Greatness.

FROM ME TO YOU Volume 1

simplebooklet.com/frommetoyouvolume1

Scan QR Code and
receive your
**Digital Copy** of
FROM ME TO YOU.

Scan QR Code and
D**ownload**
**Soundtrac**k for
FROM ME TO YOU.

# FROM ME TO YOU

Made in the USA
Middletown, DE
10 May 2022

65583399R00086